REMEMBERING OUR PASTS

by G. L. Perkins

Editorial Offices: Glenview, Illinois • Parsippany, New Jersey • New York, New York
Sales Offices: Needham, Massachusetts • Duluth, Georgia • Glenview, Illinois
Coppell, Texas • Ontario, California • Mesa, Arizona

There are more than 294 million people living in the United States. Do you ever wonder where all these people have come from? Most are **immigrants**, people who have moved here from other countries. Some immigrants came to the United States a long time ago. Others have come more recently. There are still people immigrating to this country today. The United States is a place where people from many different cultures live together.

My name is Malik. My family came from Somalia. My friend Sofía's family originally came from El Salvador. Sofía and I are in the same class at school. These are the stories about our families and how they came to live in the United States.

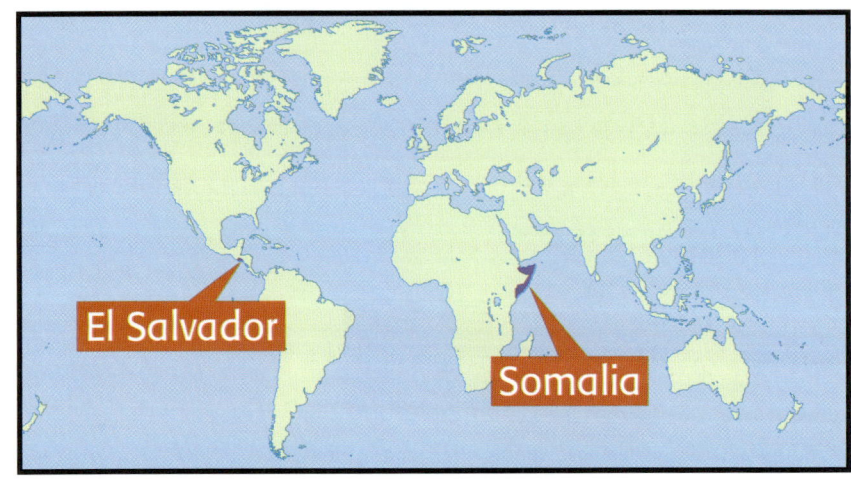

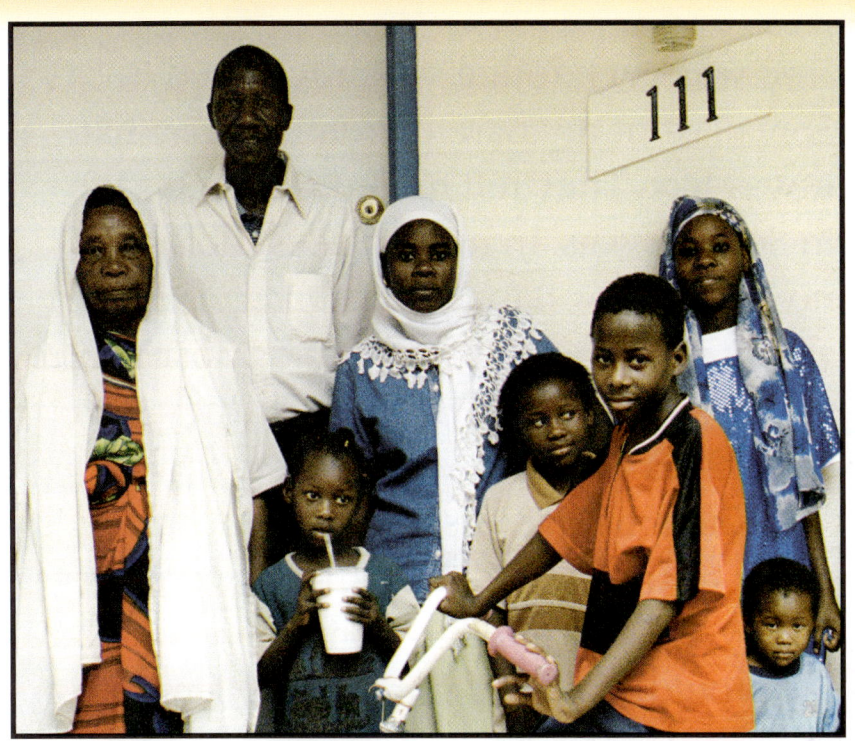

Malik's Story

My family is from an African country called Somalia. Somalia is on the eastern coast of Africa and is about the size of Texas. Most of the people in the southern part of Somalia, including my family, are known as Bantu. Bantu people come from many different African countries and have many differences. My family speaks a language called Maay Maay (my—my), but that is only one of many languages spoken by Bantu people.

I was very young when we lived in Somalia, but my parents remember what it was like. They tell me how difficult life in Somalia was. In most places there are no schools for Bantu children, and jobs for adults are very difficult to find. Most Bantu families run small farms so that they have enough to eat.

When my parents had an opportunity to come to the United States, they were very happy. They wanted to come here so that life would not be so hard. In the United States they could find better jobs and I could attend school.

Before we left Somalia, people came to talk to my parents and other Bantu immigrants about what life would be like in the United States. In Somalia we did not have some things that many people in the United States use every day. For example, in Somalia there is no formal banking system. Instead of grocery stores, we have outdoor markets. The clothing we wore was very different from what people in the United States wear. My parents knew it was going to be a big change.

When we finally arrived in the United States, we were excited but also a little scared. Everything was so different! We soon realized how much we had to learn. Some people helped my family find a place to live and answered some of the questions we had about our new country. Everything seemed very strange to us! In Somalia my family did not have things such as washers and dryers or telephones. We had to learn how to use these things.

My parents took classes to learn English. After several months my father was able to get a job at a local warehouse. He says that the job helps him learn English because he gets to practice speaking it every day!

I am learning English at school. I am also learning about the customs of the United States. I learned about the **holiday** called Independence Day, when the United States signed its Declaration of Independence, and the **custom** of celebrating with parades and fireworks. Much about this country still seems strange, but my parents remind me that by being in the United States, I will have many wonderful opportunities that I would not have had if we had stayed in Somalia.

There are some new customs that I really like. I am learning how to play baseball from my friends at school, and it is lots of fun! I would not have learned about baseball if we had not come here. I am glad that I have a chance to go to school and learn so much.

My family is getting used to all of the new things in the United States. Now that we have been here for several years, the things that were so different when we first arrived finally seem familiar to us. My parents often remind me how lucky we are to live in the United States.

Sofía's Story

I am Sofía. I was born in the United States, but my ancestors are from El Salvador. El Salvador is part of Central America, the area between North America and South America. El Salvador is a small country and is best known for its coffee crops. It has a tropical climate with rainy and dry seasons. El Salvador is known as the Land of Volcanoes because it has several active volcanoes. Earthquakes also happen from time to time. Both the volcanoes and earthquakes are scary and often damage buildings.

Life in El Salvador was difficult for my grandparents. They worked very hard, but did not earn much money. My grandparents had my father, and they wanted a better life for their son. They decided to come to the United States.

My grandparents packed everything they owned, said good-bye to their families, and headed north. It was a long journey from El Salvador to Los Angeles, California, but they knew the trip would be worth it.

My grandparents were very happy when they finally arrived in the United States. Life would be very different for them, but they met other people from El Salvador who helped them find a place to live.

In El Salvador my grandparents spoke Spanish. They knew that one of their biggest challenges would be learning English.

The jobs that my grandparents were able to get were hard work. My grandmother worked as a cook in a restaurant, and my grandfather worked at a laundromat. They worked hard and were often tired, but they were doing it to give their son a better life.

My father saw how hard his parents worked and understood that it was important for him to get a good education. He worked hard in school and learned English quickly. At home his parents spoke Spanish, so my father learned both languages. When he finished high school, my father was able to get a scholarship for college. While at college, he met my mother. Her family was also from Central America, and they had a lot in common.

Soon after they graduated from college, my parents were married. Because they worked so hard in school, they were able to get good jobs. My mother is a nurse at a hospital, and my father is a businessman. He owns a restaurant that specializes in food from Central America. People in the neighborhood like his restaurant because they can get food that reminds them of El Salvador.

My parents have learned quite a bit about the different cultures in this country. We celebrate holidays from both countries and are proud of our history. We feel that we have the best of both worlds!

My family is very close. We often go to visit my grandparents. They tell us stories about El Salvador and remind us how lucky we are to be living in the United States. I am grateful to my grandparents for making the journey here so that we could have so many opportunities.

I work hard in school so that I can go to college too. I love animals and think I would like to be a veterinarian some day.

People in the United States come from hundreds of other countries, and each person brings his or her own family history and culture. There are many reasons why people leave their own countries and come to the United States, but many people come hoping for a better life.

As you can see from our stories, it is not always easy to start over in a new place. It is wonderful to live in a country where you can meet people from many different backgrounds and where people are free to celebrate the culture of their ancestors.

Glossary

custom a special way that a group does something

holiday a special day

immigrant a person who settles in a new country